Presented to:

_____

From:

_____

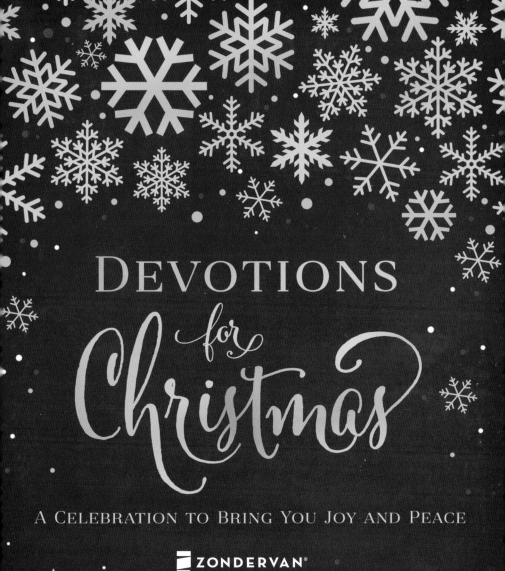

DEVOTIONS
for
Christmas

A CELEBRATION TO BRING YOU JOY AND PEACE

ZONDERVAN®

Cover design: Adam Hill

Interior design: Mallory Collins

Printed in China

16 17 18 19 20 21 22 DSC 8 7 6 5 4 3 2 1

Focusing on Jesus

*Let us . . . [keep] our eyes on Jesus, the
source and perfecter of our faith.*

<small>HEBREWS 12:1–2 HCSB</small>

Have you noticed that Christmas seems to show up in stores earlier each year? Many stores have had Christmas decorations on display since September, right next to the Halloween costumes and fall wreaths. Coffee shops were already selling gingerbread lattes when it was still eighty degrees outside. Why is there this insane rush from one holiday to the next?

Did you know there is actually a term for this blending of holidays? It's called *hallothanksmas*. Now, that's frightening. Can we all agree that our grandmothers would not have approved of hallothanksmas? If we were honest, we'd probably admit that we don't enjoy it all that much ourselves. It's just so easy to get carried away with activity this time of year. And we don't always know how to slow it all down.

But there is a way to step off the crazy train and reclaim

Christmas. What's the secret? Having a singular focus. We can choose to not rush the celebration of Christ's birth. This December, join me in focusing each day on Him—as Paul said, on the "source and perfecter of our faith." Even though at this very moment the stores are enticing us to focus on decorations, gifts, and holiday treats, let's purposefully heed Paul's advice and keep our eyes on Jesus.

We may have already gotten caught up in hallothanksmas, but that's okay. It's not too late to take back December. We can stop looking ahead to the next thing and, instead, fix our gaze on what is before us. How nice would it feel to take a deep breath and focus on the blessing of a baby born in a manger to save us from our sins? For the remainder of this holiday season, let us move forward in joy, giving Christ our full attention.

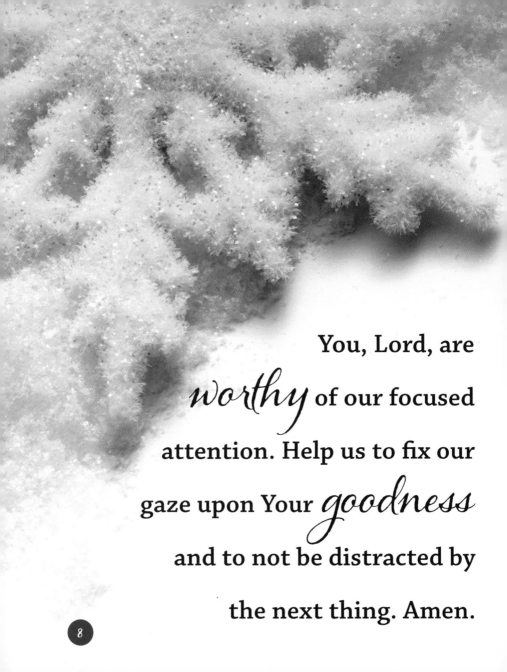

You, Lord, are *worthy* of our focused attention. Help us to fix our gaze upon Your *goodness* and to not be distracted by the next thing. Amen.

The people who walked in darkness
    have seen a great light;
those who dwelt in the land of deep darkness,
    On them had light shone. . . .
For unto us a child is born,
    to us a son is given;
and the government shall be upon his shoulder,
    and his name shall be called
Wonderful Counselor, Mighty God,
    Everlasting Father, Prince of Peace.
Of the increase of his government and of peace
    there will be no end,
on the throne of David and over His kingdom,
    to establish it and uphold it
with justice and righteousness
    from this time forth and forevermore.
The zeal of the LORD of hosts will do this.

Isaiah 9:2, 6–7

DECEMBER 2

Surprise Packaging

He had no form or majesty that we should look at him, and no beauty that we should desire him.

ISAIAH 53:2

*H*ariett has a real gift when it comes to gift wrapping. She's given concert tickets tucked inside empty cereal boxes and jewelry disguised in old coffee cans. No empty container is off-limits. Hariett takes great joy in surprising people with off-beat packaging, and they never guess what's inside. What about you? Do you judge presents by the packaging? Have you ever been surprised by what was inside?

The children of Israel were anticipating the coming of the Messiah, and they had a certain image in their minds. They were awaiting the arrival of a military leader who would show up on the scene with a lot of fanfare. They were expecting someone who would demand attention and respect by his very presence. Can you imagine their confusion when the Christ child made His humble entrance into the world?

From the very beginning Christmas has been about precious gifts in unexpected packaging. The Son of God entered

our world clothed in the flesh of an infant. God's plan to redeem and restore His people began with a newborn's cry. It was the ultimate surprise gift.

Scripture is full of God's choosing to wrap gifts in mysterious ways. From the heart of a king hidden inside of a shepherd boy to the Messiah in a manger to angels disguised as strangers, He is full of beautiful surprises. Let's not miss a single one of them! It's so easy to get caught up in appearances. We make snap judgments about people, about events in our lives, about the reasons why something seems to have happened. But when we do that, we can miss out on the best gifts. That grouchy neighbor could end up being a lifesaver, that loss of a job could be an opening to a new path, and if you're Hariett's friend, that Crisco can could hold something you just might like. Let's ask God to open our eyes to the beautiful surprises that are all around us.

I am so *thankful*, Lord, that You came the way You did. Thank You for *teaching* us to see beyond the wrapping to the *beautiful* gift inside, amen.

DECEMBER 3

Heavenly Peace

Glory to God in the highest heaven, and on earth
peace to those on whom his favor rests.

LUKE 2:14 NIV

L et's face it: Christmas can be a stressful time. We get caught up in trying to create the perfect holiday for our families. We worry about family members not getting along or the mashed potatoes being too lumpy. Before we know it, we find ourselves longing for a little of the peace we hear about in Christmas carols. Can you relate? Has your holiday season become so full of pressure that you wonder if peace is even possible?

When Christmas rolled around in 1914, World War I was in full swing. Though Pope Benedict XV suggested a temporary cease-fire in honor of the holiday, the warring countries refused to make it official. Peace did not seem to be anywhere in sight.

When the holiday arrived, the soldiers themselves chose to lay down their weapons in honor of Christmas. It was the first

reprieve in months; the sound of gunfire was replaced with the sound of singing. Enemies were reported to have exchanged gifts and played games. Though the war was far from over, the Christmas truce of 1914 brought a little peace in the midst of conflict.

What conflict are you dealing with this Christmas? Is there family drama, a financial struggle, or a health concern? No matter the specific circumstance, Christ has promised His peace to you. Peace is always available for those of us who love Him. Our holidays do not have to be marked by stress and conflict. We can quit holding on to old grudges. We can let go of envy, worry, and fear. Let's take Christmas back. This year, let's choose peace.

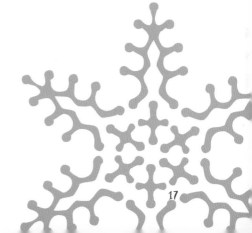

There is no *peace* to be found in accomplishments, popularity, or wealth. *True* peace is only *found* in Your presence, Jesus. Thank You, Lord, for the peace of *Christmas*, amen.

Now in the sixth month the angel Gabriel was sent by God to a city of Galilee named Nazareth, to a virgin betrothed to a man whose name was Joseph, of the house of David. The virgin's name was Mary. And having come in, the angel said to her, "Rejoice, highly favored one, the Lord is with you; blessed are you among women!"

But when she saw him, she was troubled at his saying, and considered what manner of greeting this was. Then the angel said to her, "Do not be afraid, Mary, for you have found favor with God. And behold, you will conceive in your womb and bring forth a Son, and shall call His name JESUS. He will be great, and will be called the Son of the Highest; and the Lord God will give Him the throne of His father David. And He will reign over the house of Jacob forever, and of His kingdom there will be no end."

Then Mary said to the angel, "How can this be, since I do not know a man?"

And the angel answered and said to her, "The Holy Spirit will come upon you, and the power of the Highest will overshadow you; therefore, also, that Holy One who is to be born will be called the Son of God. Now indeed, Elizabeth your relative has also conceived a son in her old age; and this is now the sixth month for her who was called barren. For with God nothing will be impossible."

Then Mary said, "Behold the maidservant of the Lord! Let it be to me according to your word." And the angel departed from her.

Luke 1:26–38 NKJV

DECEMBER 4

Family Traditions

Jesus Christ is the same yesterday and today and forever.

HEBREWS 13:8 NIV

Have you ever seen the movie *Christmas with the Kranks*? When faced with a loss of traditions, the Krank family takes drastic measures and cancels Christmas!

We might not go to such extremes, but we all have traditions that are near and dear to our hearts. The familiar smell of cider on the stove or the sound of a favorite Christmas carol can bring warmth and comfort to our holiday. What about you? What traditions can make or break your holiday season? Now, imagine someone changing them a bit. Perhaps someone tries something new with your tried-and-true recipe or suggests a new location for the holiday meal. Our traditions bring us such warmth and stability that any change to them can sting. Or we might be like the Kranks and feel like giving up altogether!

For those of us who find comfort in consistency, there is good news. Our holidays may not always look the same, but

we can still celebrate the Christ who never changes. Jesus will always be who He has always been. Scripture shows us that Jesus has been consistent in His compassion, His character, and His commands. James said that Christ "does not change like shifting shadows" (James 1:17 NIV).

Traditions are meaningful and create beautiful memories for our families, but perhaps we can add some flexibility this year. We could leave a little room for the inevitable changes of life. This may mean that we loosen our grip on Grandma's sweet potato pie recipe, and that's okay. Who knows what new joys may come along with new changes? Let's make this Christmas the year we choose Christ over our traditions.

Thank You, Lord, for the consistency of *Christmas*. In a world where feelings fade and people change, Christmas is a *beautiful* reminder of the Savior who is *always* the same, amen.

Pure as New Snow

*You were ransomed . . . with the precious blood of
Christ, like that of a lamb without blemish or spot.*

1 PETER 1:18–19

*W*hat is your first thought when snow falls for the first time each year? For many of us, our instinct is to rush outside and gather that fresh, pure snow; bring it inside; and add a little vanilla, milk, and sugar. If done correctly, the end result is a winter treat known as *snow cream.* If, by chance, you are not familiar with snow cream, there is really only one hard-and-fast rule. Only the purest snow will do. Just say no to snow with spots or blemishes.

All throughout the Old Testament, people sought purity—to be made clean as new snow. The psalmist pleaded to God, "Purify me from my sins, and I will be clean; wash me, and I will be whiter than snow" (Psalm 51:7 NLT). God's people made sacrifices in an attempt to be right with Him. They would offer lambs, doves, or whatever the Law prescribed for their situation. The problem was

that these offerings were only temporary. Because the animals were imperfect sacrifices, another sacrifice would soon be needed to cover new sins. A pure offering wasn't available.

Fortunately, God always had a plan for the redemption of His people, and it involved a pure and perfect sacrifice: His Son. Christ was not just a precious baby. He was the Lamb without spot or blemish. He came to be the sacrifice once and for all because only the purest offering would suffice to make us right with God.

This Christmas, let's remember why He came and give our thanks to Him. The cradle was always about the cross. As we think about Jesus as a baby, let's not be afraid to look ahead to His purpose in coming. Christ came because only the purest sacrifice would do.

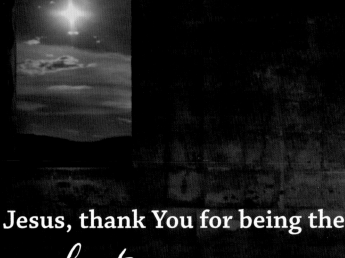

Jesus, thank You for being the *perfect* sacrifice. Thank You for doing for *us* what we could not do for *ourselves*, amen.

An Ordinary Christmas

In the same region there were shepherds out in the field, keeping watch over their flock by night.

LUKE 2:8

*I*sn't Christmas the perfect time to flex a little creative muscle? Dreams of sugarplum-frosted trees and perfect parties fill our heads. We plot and plan the perfect gifts. We outdo ourselves with new cookie recipes and leaf through magazines, looking for spectacular displays to re-create at home. It can be so much fun that, in our attempts to pull together something extraordinary, we spend a great deal of money, time, and energy on all the details. Creating an impressive Christmas can be exhausting, but there is good news. There is beauty to be found in an ordinary Christmas too.

It was just an ordinary night for the shepherds in Bethlehem. They were doing exactly what shepherds normally did in the very same place they normally grazed their flocks. Then, right in the middle of their evening, angels appeared, proclaiming the

birth of the Savior. God invaded their regular night with His holiness, and they were never the same.

We do not need to create something extraordinary for God to show up. He sent angels to shepherds in a field. Zechariah, a priest, was performing his duties in the temple when the angel Gabriel appeared to him. Jesus' first disciples were fishing when they were called to follow Him. Do you see a pattern? God shows Himself to ordinary people who are doing ordinary things. He knows where to find us, and when He does, beautiful things happen.

We all want our holidays to be special. The thing to remember is that special does not have to be stressful. It's perfectly fine to crave a little ordinary this Christmas. Let's gather around a fireplace with some hot cocoa and thank Him for the beauty that is found in an ordinary life.

We do not need to *create* a spectacle to catch Your *attention*, Lord. Faithfulness is what You seek. Help us to find Your *beauty* in the ordinary, amen.

We Three Kings

We three kings of Orient are;
Bearing gifts we traverse afar,
Field and fountain, moor and mountain,
Following yonder star.

O star of wonder, star of light,
Star with royal beauty bright,
Westward leading, still proceeding,
Guide us to thy perfect light.

Glorious now behold Him arise;
King and God and sacrifice;
Alleluia, alleluia!
Earth to heav'n replies.

DECEMBER 7

Saving Room for Dessert

When they had brought their boats to land,
they left everything and followed him.

LUKE 5:11

I f there is ever a meal when you are tempted to overeat, it's Christmas dinner. It's hard to convince yourself that one more helping of mashed potatoes could ever be a bad idea. But at some point, you might realize all those second helpings were a terrible mistake. This is usually right about the time someone asks you if you saved room for dessert. As good as those extra mashed potatoes might have been, a piece of pumpkin pie would have been even better. Can you relate? Have you ever overindulged and, as a result, missed out on something better?

When Jesus called the first disciples, they were busy living their lives. Luke 5 describes a group of fishermen who were washing their nets at that very moment, disappointed by a poor catch. Jesus taught them for a short while, and then He told them to cast their nets again. Miraculously, the nets came up

completely full! At that moment the fishermen could have stayed and enjoyed the benefits of Jesus' visit. They would have made a lot of money at market and filled their bellies for some time. But they would have missed out on the far greater blessing of walking side by side with the Savior. They made the wise decision and "left everything and followed him."

We all have certain things that give us the illusion of fulfillment. We may think wealth or fame or a certain relationship will bring us satisfaction. If we aren't careful, we will fill ourselves with the things of this world when God has far better things in store. Gorging on the world's offerings can leave us wishing we had chosen more wisely, but the way of Christ never leads to regret. As we pick and choose what we put "on our plates" this day, may we carefully consider whether each thing brings true fulfillment.

Teach us to wait *patiently* for You, Lord. May we not fill *ourselves* with the things of this world. Give us an appetite for things of *God*. Amen.

"But you, Bethlehem Ephrathah,
Though you are little among the thousands of Judah,
Yet out of you shall come forth to Me
The One to be Ruler in Israel,
Whose goings forth are from of old,
From everlasting." . . .

And He shall stand and feed His flock
In the strength of the Lord,
In the majesty of the name of the Lord His God;
And they shall abide,
For now He shall be great
To the ends of the earth;
And this One shall be peace.

Micah 5:2, 4–5 NKJV

Christmas Lights

When they saw the star, they rejoiced exceedingly with great joy.

MATTHEW 2:10

One family in New York holds the Guinness World Record title for the most lights in a residential Christmas display. Over the course of a couple of months, this family hangs more than six hundred thousand lights in every variety you could imagine. People drive from miles around to see the fantastic display glowing in the night.

What kind of light displays bring out the kid in you each Christmas? Are they multicolored or white? Are they big bulbs, little bulbs, or icicle lights? Do they stay on or blink? We may have different preferences, but we can all agree that twinkling lights add plenty of cheer to the dark, cold nights this time of year. In fact, the very first Christmas began with a light shining in the sky. When the wise men saw the star, they referred to it as "his star" (Matthew 2:2), because many years earlier a prophet had prophesied that a star would announce the birth of a king (Numbers 24:17). From the very beginning God has been dispelling darkness both literally and in our hearts.

What areas of darkness do you struggle with? We all have secrets or pains that we try to keep hidden. We may think it is better not to show our struggles, but the truth is that shame flourishes in the dark. God's desire for His people is that we would walk in the light and live in freedom. This is why Jesus refers to Himself as the light of the world in John 8:12.

Let's be like the wise men this Christmas and seek the light of Christ. Through prayer and confession, we can open up our most personal troubles to God and receive His healing and hope. We were never meant to live in darkness, and Christmas is the perfect time to leave it behind. When you're putting up lights this year, hang an extra strand to remind you that God's light chases the darkness away.

The dark is no *place* for Your people, Lord. Thank You for *shining* Your light into our lives so we can see another *way*, amen.

DECEMBER 9

An Unexpected Gift

*It has been given to you on Christ's behalf not only
to believe in Him, but also to suffer for Him.*

Philippians 1:29 HCSB

According to a January 2015 *Time* magazine article, Britain's royal family receives an odd assortment of gifts each year. Some of the most unusual were twelve boxes of mangos for Prince Andrew, a PhD thesis for Charles and Camilla, and even a pair of giant turtles given to Queen Elizabeth. What is the most surprising gift you have received? Have you ever opened a present and thought, *What in the world were they thinking?*

When we accept Christ as Savior and choose to follow Him, we also receive gifts—and they are perfectly suited for us and for God's plan. We are promised His peace, comfort, and joy. We have the gift of His presence and guidance. There are innumerable blessings in following Him. Yet we are also promised trials and tribulation. According to Paul, we receive the gifts of believing and suffering at the same time.

Whether we are serving or suffering, we get to do it for Christ. That is a gift. Are we ever closer to Him than in a time of suffering? Pastor and teacher John Piper said it this way: "There is more of God to be had in times of suffering than any other time." And who wouldn't want to have more of God?

None of us wants to ask God for suffering. It is certainly nothing that we would add to our Christmas wish lists. Yet if we walk with Christ, suffering will come. Let's pray that we will accept suffering with thankful hearts when it comes, knowing that God will work it out for His glory.

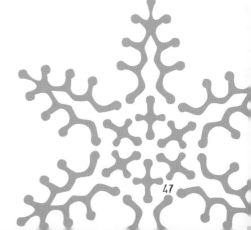

Suffering scares us, Lord.
Give us *whatever*
we need to endure faithfully
and in a way that
honors You, amen.

Home for the Holidays

*Joseph also went up from Galilee, from the town of Nazareth,
to Judea, to the city of David, which is called Bethlehem,
because he was of the house and lineage of David.*

LUKE 2:4

The days leading up to Christmas are some of the busiest travel days of the year. Soon the roads will be filled with people heading home for the holiday. We will load up the minivan and make the journey, knowing that home waits at the other end. What sights and sounds say "home" to you? For many of us, Christmas is Mama's macaroni salad. It is listening to Dad's story about that time he was stuck in Detroit on Christmas Day because of a snowstorm. We go home for the holidays because where we come from is part of who we are.

The days leading up to the birth of Christ found Joseph and his family traveling home to Bethlehem. All the people had to return to their hometowns for a census, which was just in time for Jesus' birth. Where Joseph came from and, ultimately, where Jesus came from mattered in the grand plan of God. Jesus' home

was the fulfillment of prophecies that foretold that the Messiah would be from the house of David and that He would be born in Bethlehem. Joseph's return home was a perfectly orchestrated part of God's plan.

Home is different things for different people. Perhaps you don't have those fond memories of smoked turkey and handmade gifts. But where you come from still matters, friend, because you come from the very heart of God. God dreamed up every detail of you before you were born, and He is working your origins, your past, present, and future, together as part of His grand plan. And if Christ is your Savior, your future includes a journey to a new, eternal home in heaven. We can spend this holiday looking heavenward in our hearts, knowing one day we will all truly be home for the holidays.

One day, Lord, we will all be home in Your *presence*. We long for that glad reunion day, and we *thank* You for guiding our lives as we get *there*, amen

DECEMBER 11

Seated at the Table

One of the Pharisees asked him to eat with him, and he went into the Pharisee's house and reclined at the table.

LUKE 7:36

*W*ould you be surprised to know that a traditional Christmas meal in the Czech Republic involves fried carp? If you were invited to a holiday meal in Peru, you would probably find a roast turkey stuffed with ground beef and peanuts. For most of us, Christmas dinner traditions are sacred. We want to see Mama's chestnut stuffing and Aunt Dee's sweet potato casserole just as we do every year. Much planning and preparation go into Christmas dinner, and for the most part, nobody wants any surprises.

Throughout Christ's ministry He was often seated at a table, dining with a surprising variety of individuals. People have always mattered to Him. The most important part of any meal was not what was served on the table but who was seated at the table. When the sinful woman interrupted the Pharisee's meal to

wash Jesus' feet with a fragrant oil in Luke 7, Christ welcomed her without hesitation because she mattered more than custom or tradition.

Perhaps there are people in our circles of influence who are upsetting the balance of the way things have always been done. Will we, like Jesus, offer them a seat at our Christmas table? This may be literal, meaning that our meals look different than they did in years past, with new faces, new dishes, or new circumstances. Or it may be figurative, meaning that our attitudes must change so we can value people's hearts more than we do the traditions we cling to. Let's welcome interruptions without hesitation and not be afraid to make room at the table this holiday.

Forgive us, Lord, for making our plans more of a *priority* than we make people. Send people our way, and we will *offer* them a seat at our table, amen.

Now there were in the same country shepherds living out in the fields, keeping watch over their flock by night. And behold, an angel of the Lord stood before them, and the glory of the Lord shone around them, and they were greatly afraid. Then the angel said to them, "Do not be afraid, for behold, I bring you good tidings of great joy which will be to all people. For there is born to you this day in the city of David a Savior, who is Christ the Lord. And this will be the sign to you: You will find a Babe wrapped in swaddling cloths, lying in a manger."

And suddenly there was with the angel a multitude of the heavenly host praising God and saying:

"Glory to God in the highest,
And on earth peace, goodwill toward men!"

Luke 2:8–14

DECEMBER 12

Hot Apple Cider

> *"Let not your hearts be troubled.*
> *Believe in God; believe also in me."*
>
> JOHN 14:1

Think about some seasons in your life when you faced particularly trying times. What brought comfort to your soul? What are some of the little things that warmed your heart? During this winter season there isn't much that brings comfort quite like a cup of hot apple cider. The smell of it simmering on the stove or the feel of the warm mug in our hands makes our hearts happy. That comfort is never more needed than when we have been out in the cold.

We all go through times in our lives when the world seems just a little bit colder. We experience loss and heartache. For many people the holidays can be a challenging time because they are reminded of what they've lost. While we may try to cheer them up or make things better, Christ is the true source of comfort. He is the One who can bring true warmth into a chilly world.

When Jesus spoke the words in John 14:1, He was comforting His disciples after informing them that He would be leaving. They were focusing on their loss, but He wanted them to focus on Him. We can take comfort through the coldest season by keeping our gaze on Christ and on the hope of resurrection and restoration. Paul referred to God as the God of all comfort (2 Corinthians 1:3), and He is still that for us today.

Whom do you know who needs a little comfort this Christmas? It might even be you. Let's remind ourselves and those around us that Christ is the ultimate source of comfort. Let His mercy and compassion flow through us in our prayers, sympathetic words, and in small acts of love. Hot apple cider is never a bad idea either.

You, Lord, bring *warmth* and comfort in the midst of a cold world. *Teach* us to turn to You and be warmed by Your *love*, amen.

Unwrapping the Mystery

Beyond all question, the mystery from which true
godliness springs is great: He appeared in the flesh.

1 TIMOTHY 3:16 NIV

The days leading up to Christmas are full of mystery and excitement. Packages of all shapes and sizes are under the tree. Small treasures are sticking out of the tops of stockings. Children try to guess what each present holds. Most adults are content to let the suspense remain a little longer. What about you? Do you enjoy surprises, or do you tell people exactly what you want for Christmas?

On more than one occasion, Paul referred to Christ and the gospel as a mystery. One of the greatest aspects of this mystery is that God would put on flesh and live among us. This was certainly not the way God's people had envisioned the coming of the Messiah. Yet it was exactly how He needed to come in order to ransom His people. We got the very thing we didn't even

know we needed—because God knows us better than we know ourselves.

The mystery of Christ is still being unwrapped. We only know part of His work on earth and His plan for humanity, but one day all will be revealed (1 Corinthians 13:12). While it's tempting to want to know all the answers, why not embrace the wonder of it all? There are some things we were not meant to know, and that's okay. After all, God's "understanding has no limit," while ours certainly does (Psalm 147:5 NIV). We can study, question, and seek answers, but let's not lose the wonder of God's infinitely transcendent plan. There is no need to rush things. Rest in God's perfect timing. He will finish unwrapping the mystery of Christ's coming, and we will be overwhelmed with joy.

We long to know every part of You, Lord, but *You* are more than our human minds can *comprehend.* Teach us to seek You and to lose ourselves in the *mystery* of You, amen.

A Christmas List

All the promises of God find their Yes in him.

2 CORINTHIANS 1:20

*A*ccording to the United States Postal Service, they receive millions of letters addressed to Santa each year. That's a lot of children making requests for things that they might not receive. Do you remember making a Christmas list as a kid? Every television commercial and store circular had us running to add just one more item. Nothing seems off-limits when you're a child at Christmastime. But the Christmas-morning reality was that most of us did not receive every item we requested. We can all think of that one thing that, for whatever reason, we just didn't get.

God has something for us that's much better than Christmas wishes; Scripture is full of *promises*. From Genesis to Revelation, the Bible describes more than three thousand promises from God to His people. The beauty in God's list of promises is that there is no need to rank them to indicate which things we *really*

want. He will not randomly choose which promises to keep. None of God's promises will be left unfulfilled. They all find their *Yes* in Christ.

Whether in reference to His place of birth, His lineage, or His sacrificial death, Christ kept every one of God's promises. He is the fulfillment of every prophecy. He is the answer to every prayer. Because of Christmas, we know that God always keeps His Word and that nothing is off-limits or impossible with Him.

What is your heart's desire this Christmas? What is that thing that you are almost afraid to hope for? We all have something. Let's trust God with it. Our prayers do not go out into the void but rather to our Father, who loves and cares for us. Let's leave it up to Him, knowing that God desires what's best for us and answers every prayer in His time and in His way.

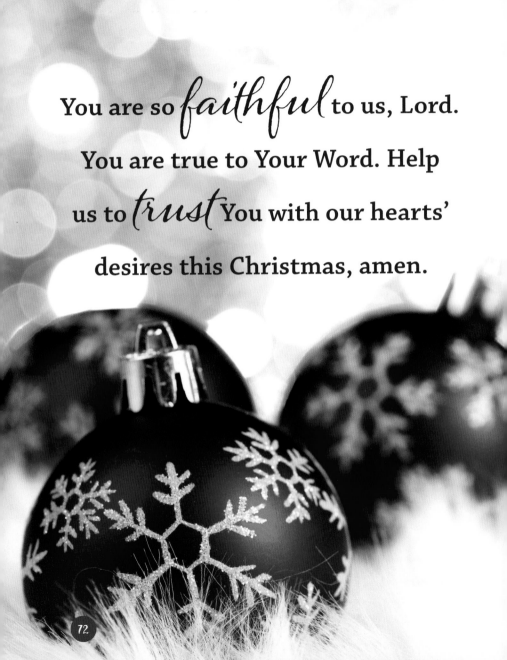

You are so *faithful* to us, Lord. You are true to Your Word. Help us to *trust* You with our hearts' desires this Christmas, amen.

DECEMBER 15

Holiday Memories

But Mary treasured up all of these things,
pondering them in her heart.

LUKE 2:19

*W*hat is your favorite Christmas ornament? What memory is attached to it? For most of us, the most loved ornaments have memories tied to them. They are the angels our grandmothers crocheted or the stars our children made from Popsicle sticks. One of the best parts of Christmas is taking the decorations out of their storage containers and, one by one, reliving the sweet memories we have treasured up over the years.

When the shepherds arrived at the manger, there was much excitement. Immediately following the angels' visit in the field, they had traveled with haste to the place where Jesus was born. Upon arriving, they told everyone all that had happened and all that the angels had to say. Luke wrote that all who heard it wondered at what the shepherds told them. And Mary took it all in and pondered it in her heart as if she didn't want to forget

a thing. While others were bustling with excitement, Mary was making memories.

Christmas can be a hectic time for many of us. We get caught up in meals, shopping, and all the festivities that accompany the holiday. We move with haste from one activity to another and, if we aren't careful, end up exhausted and empty at the end of it all. Let's do it differently this year. Instead of scurrying around, let's look around. Let's take note of the giggles of the children and smile at Grandpa napping in the chair. Let's leave the dirty dishes and instead sit around with loved ones, sharing stories. Years from now, these memories will be the treasures that we cherish time and time again.

Help us to *treasure* up what matters, Lord. Teach us the value of *memories* over material things, amen.

DECEMBER 16

Real Christmas Trees

"This people honors me with their lips,
but their heart is far from me."

MATTHEW 15:8

*A*rtificial Christmas trees date all the way back to the 1800s. It wasn't until the 1960s and the introduction of the aluminum tree that they became popular in the United States. Take a moment and picture the Christmas tree of your childhood. Was it a prickly artificial tree or a scented, sticky, live one?

The artificial trees of today are becoming more and more realistic. Unlike the shiny, silver ones of the '60s, today's artificial trees are designed to look just like the real thing. Many of us have walked into someone's home and been fooled into thinking that what stood in their living room was a live tree. But those of us who grew up with live trees at Christmas know that the true test is if you are still picking up pine needles in February.

The true test for Christ-followers is the condition of our hearts. During Jesus' time on earth, He had faithful followers

and angry opponents, but that was not all. The Pharisees were what you might call "the artificial faithful." They looked the part and played the part. If we had seen them in a crowd, we may have been fooled into thinking they were the real thing, but they were putting on a show. Christ was never fooled, because their selfish hearts always gave them away.

Christians do not all look the same. We are as different as the Christmas trees in our living rooms. We have different gifts, and we all have different struggles—and only God is fit to judge what's real and not real. In the end what matters is the condition of our hearts. God cares what's in them. This season, let's take time to reflect on our motivations and make sure our faith is the real thing.

Examine our *hearts*, Lord. Show us any areas where we have been *artificial* in our dealings with You or with *others*, amen.

A Modest Christmas

She gave birth to her firstborn son and wrapped
him in swaddling cloths and laid him in a manger,
because there was no place for them in the inn.

<small>LUKE 2:7</small>

"The Little Drummer Boy" is a classic Christmas song written in 1941. It's about a little boy invited to see the Christ child. Being a poor boy, he's worried about not having a suitable gift to bring to the newborn King. The little boy is far more concerned about this than Jesus is. Do you find yourself concerned in the same way this year? Have you been counting down the number of paychecks until Christmas? Are you disappointed that this may be a modest Christmas?

When God sent His Son into the world, the options were unlimited. He could have been born into a wealthy family who could have provided Him with lavish things. He could have been from a bigger town with more prestige. That is not the Christmas God chose. Christ came to humble parents and to humble circumstances.

Those very circumstances made the little drummer boy in the song feel as if he could approach Jesus. He took it all in and declared, "I am a poor boy too." Some Christmases are a little more modest than others. We have all had some lean years, and we probably did not see the beauty in them. But what if we didn't view a humble Christmas with disappointment? What if, instead, we saw it as an invitation for someone else to say, "Me too"? Whatever circumstance you find yourself in this year, don't let anything stop you from opening your heart to Jesus and to those around you. The gift of Christ is beyond price, and it is ours! A lavish Christmas celebration is not what matters. What counts is our humble worship of the King. Jesus accepts our praise no matter how "poor" we may consider it.

Thank You, Lord, for entering our *world* in such a humble way. Thank You for that first modest *Christmas* at the manger—and for giving us a gift of *infinite* value, amen.

Dropping Hints of Hope

*For the Lord G*OD *does nothing without revealing*
his secret to his servants the prophets.

AMOS 3:7

How good are you at keeping a surprise a secret? Can you keep it to the very end, or are you the type to drop hints in the hope that it will be discovered? We all know that person who nearly bursts at the seams when trying to hold something in (and some of us are that person!). From gifts to surprise guests, Christmas is a season of fun secrets.

Scripture tells us that God is a hint dropper. More than that, for those willing to listen, He shares His plan outright. There is something warm and endearing about knowing that God wanted to share details about His Son. Throughout the years He was whispering pieces of His plan to the prophets.

In Jeremiah God saw His people wandering in the darkness and whispered, "Don't give up. He's coming." He told Isaiah about the virgin birth. It's as if He just couldn't help but give

hints about what was to come. He knew He had the perfect gift to give to the world, and He wanted to prepare God's people for its delivery. Because of these holy whispers throughout history, believers were expecting Christ.

There's so much we don't know about the ways of God. Yet because of Christmas, His love for us is no secret. His hints throughout history were fulfilled in the manger. And He continues to whisper good things to his children: "For I know the plans I have for you, . . . plans for welfare and not for evil, to give you a future and a hope" (Jeremiah 29:11). May we tune our hearts to listen for God so that we do not miss the secrets He may want to whisper to us this season.

You are such a good *Father*. You reveal great things that bring our *hearts* comfort and joy, amen.

DECEMBER 19

Christmas Jammies

Nicodemus said to him, "How can a
man be born when he is old?"

JOHN 3:4

Are you familiar with the Holderness family? They became an Internet sensation by creating videos about their new Christmas jammies each year. Dressed in snowman-covered fuzzy pj's, they sing clever lyrics about their family Christmas traditions and dance around. Folks are hooked, because who doesn't love a grown man and woman wearing footed pajamas? The fabulous part is that these hilarious garments come in all sizes—because no one is too old or too big for Christmas pajamas.

Something about Christmas seems to make us young again. We can't help but experience a little childlike wonder this time of year. How sad would it be if we felt too old to throw a snowball or build a gingerbread house? In the same way, Christ's love defies age.

Nicodemus was an old man. He was familiar with Jesus' teaching and wanted to know more. Because he was a ruler of the Jews, he went to question Jesus and to make sense of everything He had said. How could it be possible for someone to be born again to see the kingdom of God? This troubled Nicodemus because he was already old—birth was a long time ago for him.

Jesus gives us good news: we are never too old to choose God and be born of the Spirit. We can have the faith of a child at any age—it's the Spirit of God that makes us new. As long as there is breath in our bodies, He can use us. There is no limit to what God can accomplish through a willing vessel. It's not too late. Someone else won't be better suited for the job. We have not missed our chance. We are not too old for God to use, or for Christmas jammies!

Use us, *Lord*. We may have the bodies of *adults*, but give us the faith of a *child*, amen.

DECEMBER 20

Christmas Stockings

"Call to me and I will answer you, and will tell you great and hidden things that you have not known."

Jeremiah 33:3

Have you ever hidden a special gift for a child deep inside the toe of a Christmas stocking? How exciting it is to watch that child pull out the rest of the candy and tiny trinkets when you know something precious is waiting at the bottom! On the other hand, consider how frustrating it is when the child is satisfied with the candy and does not seek anything beyond that initial treat. You can't wait for the moment when your child will find the greater prize.

Do you ever feel as though your life is missing something? So many of us have gratefully accepted Christ as Savior but have not taken our relationship with Him any deeper. We love Jesus, but as we meet the challenges of everyday life, we stop searching for Him. We forget God has things yet to reveal. We really are missing out on an important gift: we are missing more of Him.

Christ has hidden a destiny for us that we may know nothing

about. Yes, there is a sweetness to salvation, much like the chocolate treats at the top of the stocking. We should certainly embrace and enjoy that indescribable gift. Oh, but let's also go deeper! Gems of wisdom and gifts of strong character and hope that come through perseverance will escape our notice unless we are willing to go further with Christ.

The writer of Hebrews said that we must come to God believing that He exists *and* that He has rewards for those who diligently seek Him (Hebrews 11:6). Through the inspired words of Scripture, God is encouraging us to dig for the deeper gifts of Christ—to continue to pray, study, and serve Him with all our hearts. This Christmas, let's ask Him to reveal to us the hidden treasures that we did not even realize were ours for the taking. He is waiting for us to seek the greatest prize—Him.

We long to know You more, Lord. *Teach* us the great and hidden things that are deep within Your *heart*. Amen.

DECEMBER 21

Gift Tags

"See, I have written your name on the palms of my hands."
Isaiah 49:16 NLT

How do you like to wrap your Christmas presents? There are so many options! Some prefer paper with cartoon characters or snowmen and a nice peel-and-stick bow. Others choose a shiny, foil wrapping with an elaborate ribbon. Then there are those of us who begin with visions of beautifully wrapped packages but, somewhere around the twentieth present, pull out the gift bags and tissue paper.

Whatever presentation you choose, the last step is attaching the gift tag. You lovingly write a person's name on the tag and set the gift apart for that specific individual. It's the very last step in the whole process of thinking about, shopping for, and purchasing just the right gift. And when someone sees that gift sitting under the tree just for him or her, how special do you think that person feels?

God's love for His people is the most well-planned, extravagant

gift of all time. He went to great lengths to prove His love to us. Then, lest there be any question, the Lord tells His people that their names are engraved upon His holy hands. The gift of God's love has our names written on it, and it is ours to open and receive.

It would be terribly sad for such a precious gift to remain unopened. The Enemy would have us believe that God's gift isn't for us. He tells us we are unworthy of God's love. Do not believe it, sweet friends. God has made us worthy through His Son's sacrifice. God reaches out His hands, and they are marked with our names so we know that the gift of Christ is for us.

It's heartwarming to see our names on a *gift* tag, knowing that someone thought so much of us. Yet, no *earthly* gift compares to knowing that our *names* are written on Your hands and on Your heart. Thank You, *Lord*, for giving Your Son to us, amen.

DECEMBER 22

Christmas Letters

There is one mediator between God and men, the man
Christ Jesus, who gave himself as a ransom for all.

1 TIMOTHY 2:5–6

Beginning a couple of weeks before Christmas, many of us start to walk to our mailboxes with expectation. We know that Christmas cards and letters will arrive almost daily. Families in matching outfits will grace the covers of glossy cards. There will be postcards with brief greetings. Then there are the Christmas letters, replete with details of the past year. Whose Christmas letter do you look forward to receiving?

Christmas letters are personal things. They don't go to everyone because the message isn't for everyone. Not everyone needs to know that you've decided to go back to your natural hair color or that your little sister finally got her braces taken off. They each contain a specific message for specific people. To share someone's letter with an unintended recipient might even amount to gossip.

While some Christmas letters may not be for everyone, the story of Christmas is for every single one of us. Christ came to earth because God loved the whole world (John 3:16). Anyone can read Scripture and know that it is meant for him or her. Christ came for everyone, and He died for everyone. In today's verse Paul wrote that Christ gave Himself as a ransom for all.

It's easy to assume that everyone knows the message of the gospel, but that's not the case. People in our lives hunger and thirst for the hope of Christ, and those of us who hold fast to the Word of God must be willing to share it. You may not want to share the details of your sister's Christmas letter with the world, but the gospel isn't gossip. It's good news. Let's share it!

Your love is for *everyone,* Lord! You have made a way for everyone to *come* to You. Give us the boldness to share the *gospel* with the world, amen.

DECEMBER 23

Going Caroling

Coming up at that very hour [Anna] began to give thanks to God and to speak of him to all who were waiting for the redemption of Jerusalem.

LUKE 2:38

Have you ever gone door-to-door at Christmastime singing carols to your neighbors? Historically, caroling in England was a way of wishing one's neighbors good health, and it was not strictly a Christmas activity. It wasn't until the 1800s that Christmas carols made their way onto the song list. Caroling became a popular way to spread Christmas cheer to friends, neighbors, or those who were unable to leave their homes. Christmas was shared with the whole community.

Those who learned about the baby Messiah were quick to share good news with those around them. The shepherds went immediately to the manger to share everything the angels had spoken about the Christ child (Luke 2:17). Upon seeing Jesus in the temple, the prophetess Anna told everyone about Him (Luke 2:38). They all grasped the importance of what was taking place and sought to share it with others.

Why do you think caroling is not as prevalent these days? Are we too busy? Are we afraid it would be an imposition on others? What stops us from sharing the wonder of Christmas with those around us? No one is saying that you have to pick up some handbells and start knocking on doors. The important part is not the act of singing but the act of going.

How can we take the message of the Messiah to our neighbors? The good news is still good news after all these years. People still need to know that the Savior has come for them. You can sing if you like, or you could take a casserole or an invitation to a get-together to one of your neighbors. It doesn't matter what methods we use as long as we share the message of Christmas in our communities.

Lord, Your birth is still worth *celebrating* and sharing. Help us to take the good *news* of Your coming to those around us, amen.

DECEMBER 24

Holy Anticipation

It had been revealed to [Simeon] by the Holy Spirit that he would not die before he had seen the Lord's Messiah.

LUKE 2:26 NIV

Is there anything more exciting than Christmas Eve? Family and friends will soon be filling our homes with love and laughter. The presents that we have lovingly chosen and wrapped will finally be opened. All of our planning and preparation has brought us here, and now we wait with anticipation.

Simeon was no stranger to anticipation. The Holy Spirit promised him that he would not die before seeing the Christ. He probably woke up each morning thinking, *Today could be the day!* Every day he continued to draw breath, he waited to see the promised Messiah. That, my friends, is a life filled to the brim with anticipation.

Just as Simeon longed for Jesus' coming, we now long for Him to come again. We see promises of His return all throughout Scripture. Revelation tells us that He is currently on His way,

bringing justice and a new world (22:12). We live with the knowledge that not only will He come someday, but He could come *any day*. How exciting is that?

For those of us who long for His appearing, our days are filled with anticipation. A day is no longer just another twenty-four-hour period filled with tasks to do and errands to run. For us, every night can be like Christmas Eve. Let's greet each new day with great anticipation knowing that Jesus could arrive at any moment.

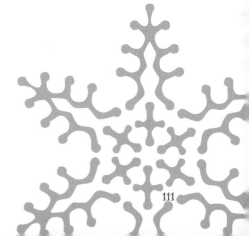

It is with great anticipation, Lord, that we *await* Your return. May we live in such a way that when You *arrive*, we can say, "Yes, Lord, we were *expecting* You," amen.

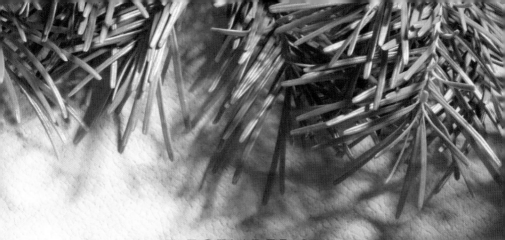

A Savior Is Born for You

Today a Savior, who is Messiah the Lord,
was born for you in the city of David.

Luke 2:11 HCSB

Would it surprise you to know that December 25 probably isn't the exact day of Jesus' birth? Many Orthodox Christians, whose churches never adopted the Gregorian calendar, celebrate Christmas on January 7. And what about the calendar year? Would it shock you to know that many biblical scholars believe Christ was born between 6 and 4 BC? We simply do not know the exact date that the angel declared, "Today a Savior . . . was born." But that isn't the most important part of the message.

Whether today ends up being a wonderful day, or if it doesn't end up as you hoped it would, the events of *today* are not the most important part of the celebration. Wherever today finds you, the message is still the same. Messiah the Lord was born *for you!* What a life-altering fact! Jesus did not come to give us

a sweet story to tell. He did not come so that we could have a reason to exchange gifts. Christmas Day is about God giving the gift of His Son to you so that you could belong to Him.

The gift is the same whether you are surrounded by family or alone in your living room. It is the same on January 7 as it is on December 25. In fact, not knowing the exact date of Christ's birth may be a gift in itself. We do not have to limit our adoration to just one day! A Savior was born for us, and that is worth celebrating any day. Today, let us commit to celebrating God's gift each day of the year.

So much about You, God,

remains a *mystery*. But

knowing You sent Jesus

to save us is *enough*.

Thank You for the gift of your

precious Son, amen.

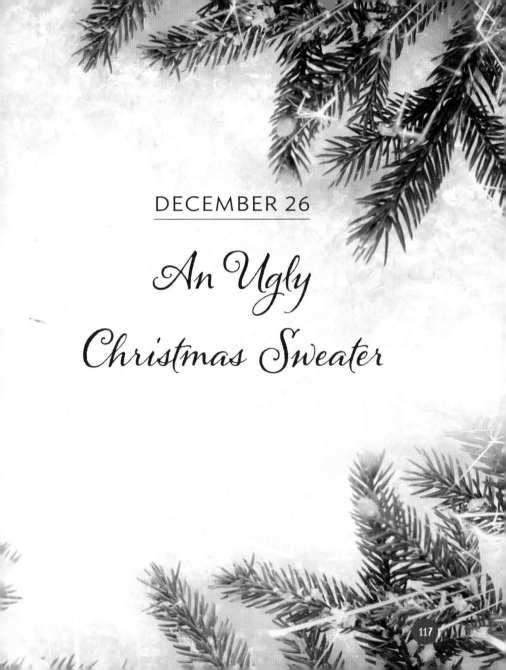

DECEMBER 26

An Ugly Christmas Sweater

Every good gift and every perfect gift is from above.
JAMES 1:17

fter weeks of fighting crowds and standing in lines, most of us are tired of being in stores of any kind. Yet, according to a *Wall Street Journal* article, hundreds of us will flock to stores to return more than $60 billion worth of merchandise in the days following Christmas. What about you? Are you making plans to return an ugly sweater or that casserole dish you know you'll never use? Did you save gift receipts for your friends and loved ones?

Some gifts just don't work out. No matter how hard we try, we do not always know what someone else wants or needs. We may think we have come up with the perfect present for someone only to see him or her standing in the return line, holding our gift. It's possible that our choices are not as perfect as we thought.

But God's gifts are different. He knows exactly what we need.

The gifts He places in our lives are good and perfect, although He has a way of giving us things that we would have never asked for or sought out for ourselves. Yet, in the end, they are always exactly right for us.

Is there something that God has placed in your life that you wouldn't mind returning? You're not alone. We do not always understand His gifts. Your struggle or misfortune may seem like an ugly sweater that surely must have been intended for someone else. But He makes no mistakes, sweet friend. Whether our trials have come as a consequence of sin, as a thorn from Satan, or as something straight from the hand of God, we can still trust that He will turn it into something good and perfect. Let's choose to accept what God allows to come our way, knowing that He will make something beautiful out of whatever we face.

When we do not *understand* Your gifts, Lord, give us the strength to trust Your *heart.* We thank You in advance for all of Your good and *perfect* gifts, amen.

Christmas Leftovers

But as for you, continue in what you
have learned and firmly believed.

2 TIMOTHY 3:14 HCSB

Raise your hand if you still have Christmas leftovers in your refrigerator. Aren't they wonderful? Not many things can beat a nice plate of leftover turkey and dressing. Whether you eat it just as you did on Christmas Day or create something brand-new with your leftovers, it's a way to keep the holidays going just a little while longer. Many people may have worked to create your Christmas meal, and you can relive that togetherness as you enjoy the containers full of delicious food. (Plus, you can enjoy not cooking for once!)

Our spiritual lives are much like a Christmas dinner. At times, our loved ones surround us and pour into our lives. Other times we are alone, but we can return to the lessons they have taught us and continue to be blessed by them. Have you ever gone through a difficult season and been reminded of a scripture someone taught you or a word of encouragement from the past? Those are spiritual leftovers, and they nourish the soul.

Paul warned Timothy that the day would come when people would begin falling away from the faith. Some would begin to doubt the things they had been told about Christ. His encouragement to Timothy in today's verse was to continue on in what he had learned. When life became chaotic or confusing, Timothy could go back to what he knew to be true.

We live in a constantly changing world. People are challenging Christian beliefs, and some are redefining scriptural truths to make them more acceptable to the world. But we do not need to repackage or "reheat" the Word of God. "For the word of God is alive and active. Sharper than any double-edged sword, it penetrates even to dividing soul and spirit, joints and marrow; it judges the thoughts and attitudes of the heart" (Hebrews 4:12 NIV). God's Word is just as perfect and true today as it was when it was first inspired.

There is *nothing* new that can compare to You, Lord. No new philosophy can *explain* or encourage the way You can. Help us to *continue* in what we have learned and firmly *believe* to be true, amen.

DECEMBER 28

The Season Continues

Going into the house they saw the child with Mary his mother, and they fell down and worshiped him.

MATTHEW 2:11

You may have seen a nativity set with three wise men standing right next to the shepherds in the stable. One might even be set up on your hearth right now, or perhaps the children in your church acted it out during Advent. This beautiful scene is ingrained on our collective Christmas memory. So while it may not have been a surprise to biblical scholars, most of us were shocked when we realized the wise men were not present at the manger. Now, before we start removing the wise men from Grandma's favorite nativity scene, let's think for a moment.

From Scripture we can surmise that it could have taken an unknown number of magi as long as two years to travel from where they were to where Christ was residing. They would have traveled by caravan and occasionally stopped for lodging. Everyone making the journey would have been very much aware that the goal was reaching the Christ child.

Today's scripture tells us that immediately upon entering the home (not the stable), they fell down to worship Him. The journey was all about Jesus. After worshiping Him, they presented the child with gifts. It was still a celebration of the birth of the Savior. Two years later, it was still Christmas.

It's common to feel a little bit of an emotional letdown following Christmas. So much effort and energy goes into the weeks leading up to it, and then it's all over so quickly. But what if it weren't? What if it continued after decorations were packed away and the leftovers were eaten? Let's linger over the Christ child a little longer. Perhaps those old nativity sets had the right idea. It is never too late or the wrong time to celebrate the birth of Christ.

Lord, You are *worthy*
of much celebration. May
we honor and *worship*
You not just at Christmastime
but *always*, amen.

DECEMBER 29

The Aroma of Christmas

For we are the aroma of Christ to God.

2 Corinthians 2:15

What does Christmas smell like to you? Candles are popular accessories in homes this time of year, since the sense of smell helps create such strong, warm memories. Candles and burners come in delicious scents, like orange, pumpkin spice, and pine tree. One large candle company even sells a candle called "Christmas Eve," which is supposed to smell like candied fruit. It's good enough to eat!

American poet Diane Ackerman once said, "Nothing is more memorable than a smell."

Nothing about God's creation is accidental. He designed our bodies so the sense of smell would be linked to our memories. Perhaps that is why Paul used the phrase "the aroma of Christ" to tell us that we are to be like a comforting scent in the memories of those we encounter.

Paul told the Corinthians that God uses believers to spread the fragrance of the knowledge of Christ everywhere. Then, in

his very next sentence, he said that *we* are the aroma of Christ to God. In other words, we should always smell like Christ, leaving traces of His peace, His joy, and His grace. Have you ever known someone whose lovely scent lingers long after he or she has left the room? When we leave someone's presence, it should be Christ's scent that lingers: the essence of His holiness and love.

Let's be intentional about the spiritual scent we leave behind. People will remember it. If we are to do everything as unto the Lord, everything we do should include the fragrance of Christ and reflect well on Him. Our interactions with others should give off a sweet aroma. And when God draws near us and takes a deep breath, live in such a way that He is filled with the scent of His Son. Let's share the aroma of Christmas.

There is no *greater* honor, Lord, than for our lives to *contain* the aroma of Christ. May the scent of our lives bring *memories* of Your Son to mind, amen.

Cradle to Cross

Then [Joseph of Arimathea] took [Jesus' body] down and wrapped it in a linen shroud and laid him in a tomb.

LUKE 23:53

hings have a way of coming full circle." That's what we say about a situation that seems to end where it began. Can you think of a situation that played out in your life in a way that made you think things had come full circle? In the study of Scripture, we would call this an *inclusio*. The book of Luke has several examples. The ministry of Jesus began with Satan in the wilderness, questioning His divinity (Luke 4:3) and ended with the rulers questioning His divinity as He hung on the cross (Luke 23:35). The very setting of Luke is an *inclusio*: the book opens and closes in the temple.

Think back to Luke 2 when Mary gave birth to Christ. As He drew in His first breaths, she wrapped Him in cloths and laid Him in the manger. Imagine the gentleness of those hands as they held the Savior and the nervousness of a new mama as she laid Him in the manger. Now, let's imagine Joseph of Arimathea

as He removed Christ's body from the cross. Imagine the gentleness of those hands as they held the body of the Savior and the nervousness of a believer as he laid Him in the tomb. Were two sets of human hands ever as blessed as those of Mary and Joseph of Arimathea?

The similarities in the way Mary and Joseph of Arimathea handled Christ's body were not coincidental. We are meant to link the cradle and the cross together in our minds. They were always part of the same circle of events. One was intended to lead to the other. As we close out another calendar year and reflect on beginnings and endings, let's not lose sight of the fact that the baby in the manger became the Man on the cross. The ending to this story spelled a new beginning for the world—and gave us new hope.

We have no adequate words, *Lord*, to thank You for Your life. Your birth, burial, and *resurrection* are gifts we treasure, amen.

DECEMBER 31

A New Thing

Therefore, if anyone is in Christ, he is a new creation.
The old has passed away; behold, the new has come.

2 CORINTHIANS 5:17

*P*ause and take a deep breath. You have made it through another Christmas season and are about to embark on a brand-new year. The gifts have all been given, and the food has all been eaten. The decorations will soon be put away. (Some of us will not have the energy to take the tree down for a little while. That's okay; this is a place of grace.) For all of us, this is a time of new beginnings. What are you looking forward to in the New Year?

All throughout Scripture, Christ created new beginnings. A young virgin girl began the journey of motherhood. Prisoners began new lives of freedom, and the lame were given new hope through His healing. He wiped away sins and sicknesses and offered fresh starts instead. Who among us could use a new beginning too?

How was this past year for you? Most of us could list a few highs and lows. We wish we could do some things over, or perhaps not do them at all. There is good news. Christ still delights in giving us new beginnings. We can move on from any mistakes we have made this year. We can allow God to heal any wounds and lead us back toward Him. We can ask Him to begin a new work in us.

Let's not enter this New Year carrying old burdens. Wouldn't we rather have new blessings instead of old baggage? This is the perfect time. Let the old pass away. In Christ we are new creations created for new things. Let's prepare our hearts to receive them.

Because of *Christmas,*

Lord, we can be made new.

Thank You, *Jesus*, that

we are not just cleaned-up

versions of our old *selves* but

brand-new creations, amen.